Loving Your Style

Learning how to birth your style and be confident with it

By SashaB

Introduction

Hey! Hey! Hey!

I know you are super excited to be learning the key elements of style. I know some say fashion, but I am speaking about style. Fashion is what you buy off of a rack, style is something you have or is something you are suppose too have. I know you see a lot of people out there showing you fashion, but I want this book to show you style. From the days you are feeling fabulous to the days you just want to be comfortable, I want to show you how to style them probably.

Yes, fashion is fabulous and fierce, and style can be the same if you do it correctly. I want to help people stop buying the complete outfits off the mannequins and buy what works for them. See this thing about style is way beyond fashion, style comes from the inside out. Which is why you see so many people draped in fashion and you look at them trying to find their style, because you know that isn't it. Like let's be honest, THAT CAN'T BE THE FINISH PROJECT OUT YOUR CLOSET! Let's be for real! People it so caught up in the fashion thing; that they forget to have fun with style. Style is what makes fashion fun, creative, amazing etc. Style is what gives fashion so much energy, because when you go purchase an item the first thing you ask yourself is "how am I going to style this."

The answer is in the pudding you are going to style it with style, not with fashion, because you just brought fashion off the rack. So, when you are purchasing fashion off the rack don't go home and add an extra layer of fashion, no, no! That's an epic fail for the fashion that you are trying to bring together. We all know fashion is the easy part, everyone has fashion; style is the part that some struggle with.

See me yes, I may purchase fashion off the rack, but I always go home and put it on with style. You know, things that work with my personality, how I feel in the garment, is it working for my body type, is the color working for my skin tone. These are things that I take into consideration before I purchase fashion off the rack, because they are extremely important. Because if I just purchase fashion off the rack without considering myself, I will have a bunch of piece that I feel uncomfortable when I wear it, something that doesn't compliment my skin tone and the worst of all something that doesn't compliment my awkward body shape. Yes, I said it… I have an awkward body shape, but it's okay because it's mine and I know how to wear things that make it look fabulous and fierce honey!

I really hope that after reading this book, you get an idea of style and how to wear fashion and make it work for you style. Because I'm telling you now, everything is not for everybody, and whoever said it was told a lie! So, let's keep off our shoes, let our hair down, and get ready to change your whole perspective on fashion and style.

Table of Contents

Loving Your Style

Learning how to birth your style and be confident with it

Book Contact
email: Lovingyourstyle29@gmail.com

Give feedback at:
Lovingyourstyle29@gmail.com

Body Symmetry

Okay ladies, as I stated in the introduction "Everything isn't for everybody", well right now I am here to tell you that's one of the realest things you will ever hear; and the proof is in the pudding. The pudding is called "symmetry", which is something everyone has, but here's the catch everyone's body symmetry is different. In this chapter we are going to learn about different body symmetries. I know in the back of your mind you are saying "I don't want to learn about my body symmetry, my body isn't flattering." Well that's wrong you just need to identify with your symmetry and learn to make it work for you. Now, please don't get afraid by the word "symmetry" it simply means proportion. So, let's all ask ourselves this question, "What is your body symmetry?"

Although there are many types of symmetry going on with the human body, there are only six of them that our body shapes reflect of. These six are; The Pear, Inverted Triangle, Rectangle, Hour Glass, Diamond and The Apple. Now, I hope after you have read them, it started to click a little more of how your body is proportioned. You know sometimes in life we all need to take that huge pill to swallow and be honest with ourselves. Now that we have taking the huge pill relax because I am here to help and tell you all about what works for your specific body symmetry.

- **Pear Shape**: means that you are small at the top and bigger at the bottom
- **Inverted Triangle**: having broad shoulders or being top heavy and smaller at the bottom
- **Rectangle Shape**: having the same size top, mid-section and bottom which creates a longer torso
- **Hour Glass**: having the same size top and bottom and a smaller waist
- **Diamond**: having a small top and bottom and a wider mid-section
- **Apple**: having a completely round top, mid-section and bottom ("36", "36", "36")

Don't be afraid to take a moment an embrace your bodies symmetry, because at the end of the day if your symmetry is something that you don't like there are ways to make it look great and I'm not speaking of plastic surgery, I'm talking about making it look great with fashion and style. See, because we really don't know how important body symmetry is where things that make us look short, stubby, bigger than we are, frumpy etc. Guess what, that stops right now! Because it's not about being a size two, it's about wearing what works for you and make you feel confident and what makes your body look great at whatever size you are.

Knowing your body symmetry helps with self-confidence, self-love and gives you that ability to be sexy in your own style instead of always trying to copy others. It is extremely important to recognize that we are all shaped differently so when we buy fashion off the rack we are buying things that work for us, that will make us feel confident, sexy, and fabulous. We are no longer buying fashion that we are unsure about or buying fashion and trying to make it work. No, No, No. We are done with that and we are moving on to bigger better style.

No matter what your body symmetry I want to show you how to make it sexy for you, because this is something that makes us unique. Also, look at it as being able to create your own sexiness that you can add or take away from. I really hope that after this book that it will help you embrace the shape that you are, give you the ability to be fabulous and fierce using your own personal style.

So, Let's Rock out to Symmetry right now!!!

Styles That Work for You

Now, that we have read about the different body symmetries and have an understanding of them, again I want to repeat embrace it and love it; and if there are some things you don't love (which I have a few) you can always change it (work on it), wear things that give your body the shape you want or wear things that make your features stand out. Everyone has a different favorite something, and everyone has a different flaw, so since this is my book and I am talking to you guys about embracing your bodies, I am going to do a little confession on my own. I absolutely hate my mid-section it's always been a struggle for me and now since the twins it has gotten worst (but I'm working on it) and I wear things to hide or make it not so noticeable.

First there is the "High Waist" denim (which I absolutely adore) because it breaks up your body and gives it a shape. It shows where the waist line is. Now when I say waist line, I am speaking about the actual waist. They also give your butt a nice shape, or the shape you want/desire. You can get "High Waist" denim in flare, boot cut, straight let and of course skinny. They will give you that great middle shape no matter what body symmetry you have.

The second, it the "Vertical Stripes", that give you height and make you look a little more-slimmer than you are. I am very big on this one because I am not the tallest person in the world so when I am going out and I want to look a little bit more on the slimmer side, you better believe that I am going for the "Vertical Stripes." Yes Lord, they work for me every single time!

Lastly, is the "Button Down" shirt, which hugs everything that you want to show and hides everything you want to hide. This is something that I have started to embrace because not only did it make me feel lady like, it also gave me that sexy top proportion that I personally wanted for myself.

Please don't get discourage and say "is this all the styles she's going to speak on" nope not at all! I just wanted to share some styles that take the stress off of my mid-section and I also want you to try them to see if they help you. But I am going to touch on a lot of styles for different body symmetries.

The Pear Shaped: You want to find tops and jackets that show off your slender upper body while also creating a fuller illusion with

the right places to achieve that will balance with the larger hops.
Tops that work for you are as follows.

- Large V-Necks or Scoop Necks
- Horizontal Stripes
- Big Lapels
- Padding or embellished shoulders
- Cropped Tops

When it comes to bottoms, you want to focus on pants and skirts
that minimize your lower either by slimming or elongation. Using
dark colors, clean and straight lines are ideal for you. Bottoms that
work for you are as follows:

- Wide-leg or straight-leg pants or denim
- A-line Skirts that are mostly fitter as the hips
- Darker Colors

The Inverted Triangle: you want to for pieces that lighten or slim
down your upper half and minimize your broad shoulders, but you
want to do this without erasing your curves and your bust. Tops
that work for you are as follows:

- V-Necks and other open necklines
- Strapless or asymmetric tops
- Empire-Waist Tops
- Large Belts

When it comes to bottoms you want to create more curves and
fullness to achieve that perfect balance to your more rounded half.
Bottoms that work for you are as follows:

- Relax-fit pants and denim with embellished or heavy
  pockets
- A-Line Skirts or other skirts that Flare out
- Boot Cut Jeans

The Rectangle: you have a relatively straight shape and smaller
bust, so you want tops that create more curves and more feminine
silhouettes by defining your waist. Tops that work best for you are
as follows:

- Fitted Blazers with shoulder pads
- Embellished or pockets are the bust and shoulders

- Top that are more flowy around the bust

When it comes to bottoms you want to add more curves and legs continuing the proportion balance between the upper and lower body. Bottoms that work for you are as follows:

- Large back pockets
- Figure hugging and low-rise jeans
- Pencil and A-line Skirts with a cinched waist

The Hourglass: having a feminine and curvy figure, ladies with an hourglass figure only need to find the right tops accent this feature without appearing heavier than they are. Tops that work for you are as follows:

- Scooped and V-necklines
- Tops that sit at the waist
- Cleaned lined jackets and coats that are well cut and fitted

When it comes to bottoms, just about all styles of bottoms look great on you, when paired with the right top that shows off your silhouette. Bottoms that work for you are as follows:

- Pencil skirts and A-line Skirts
- Jeans that are fitted around that hips and back side

The Diamond: although there are some people out there that don't believe that there are tops out there for the diamond shape body type, I have good news for you. There is a large amount of tops that the diamond body type can wear that are visually pleasing. Tops that work for you are as follows:

- Low Necklines
- Bright Colors and soft materials
- Belted waists
- Capped or puffed sleeves

When it comes to bottoms, the key is to slim down your lower body with the right pieces. Bottoms that work for you are as follows:

- Darker Colors
- Relaxed or straight fit bottoms with high or large pockets
- Straight flare or gathered skirts

The Apple: you want to find tops that enhance the volume to your bust and shoulders while emphasizing your waist-line. Tops that work for you are as follows:

- Deeper V-Necklines or wider necklines
- Nipped in waists
- Semi fitted or loose and draped
- Shirts and jackets that end at the hip

When it comes to bottoms you want to stick with the bottoms that enhance your natural curves and shape without adding extra bulkiness. Bottoms that work for you are as follow:

- Pocketed Cargo pants
- Straight or slightly flared skirts
- Bottoms that have a bit of stretch to them

How fun was that?! LOL! Ladies please don't get discouraged or think that you wear every single one of these pieces together because you don't, that's not even how style works. I just wanted to give you a general idea of what pieces would bring out your features. So, if I over whelmed you a little bit I apologize, I am going to show you how to work these pieces with your own personal style. Because, most importantly it's about Loving your own style, loving who you are and loving what you wear. What I have listed under the body symmetry categories are just pieces that will help accent what you want to show off, but again I will show and help you put them together.

So, I really hope I didn't over whelm you ladies, and that you will gladly follow me to the next chapters to see how to own your Style and how to incorporate the styles that work for you and have a finish piece that you love.

Different Denim for Different Shapes

Ladies,

So, I am sure that we are all aware of the many styles of denim, and how the denim you wear affects your body. But if you don't know what they are, I am going to name them before I started breaking them down. The different styles of denim are Flare, Bootcut, Straight and Skinny. I know that some of you have your favorite denim or your go to denim because I do, and that's fine and that's normal, but I want us to indulge a little bit more in denim and realize how special it is. I know you are reading this saying "Sasha it's just denim, how special can it really be?" Well it is extremely special because denim can change or emphasize any body type when worn correctly.

So, let's pause for a second and I am going to speak on the denim I have on right now, while I am writing a chapter on denim. I am not going to name the brand of the denim, but they're stretchy and they are skinny and they are absolutely horrible. The fabric is soft, but they have a little bit more stretch then I like. They make my butt look flat, which is the absolute no! Because I already have a flat butt so thanks skinny denim for doing more damage and not giving me justice. I brought them because they were cropped, I have a weakness for "Cropped Skinny" denim, but these I just can't get with. See how important denim is, I am over here having a break down about the denim I have on today, tomorrow I need to do better.

Now that I got that out the way back to the regular scheduled program! So, I am going to be speaking on my favorite denim first which is the flare denim! Yes, I love me some flare denim, because being an inverted triangle, flare denim add balance to my broad shoulders, which is why I love them so much. Now I must say that if I am going to wear a fitted top, I mean a tight fitted top, I am going to go in my closet and get out some flare denim. Because a, my shirt is tight fitting, so you will be able to see my body and of course my shoulders and b, having a fitted shirt doesn't take away from having the flare at the bottom of your denim.

Ladies, please don't be disappointed or scared to try flare denim, they are a great style of denim and they also work for all body types except for the Pear shape. Why, it doesn't work that well with the pear shape is because when you are pear shaped you already bigger at the bottom and flare denim is also big at the bottom, and you can't put big and big at the bottom it will just make you look bigger than what you are. Please don't get discouraged by me saying that, to all my women who are pear shaped, I do have some great denim styles that look great on you too.

I know that sometimes women get intimated by flare denim because they make an already short women look shorter, but that's only if you wear them with flats. Take my advice if you are going to wear flare denim and you are short (like me) please wear a heel. Wearing flare denim and flats only works out for tall people!

So, let's recap, when it comes to flare denim you most likely always want to go with a tight fitted top just because you want to give balance to your body symmetry and allow the flare denim to give your curves some definition. Ladies listen to me if you have been scared to try flare denim, tell yourself "today I am no longer afraid of the flare," because the flare denim is your friend!!

Now that flare is over, let's talk about another style of denim that some ladies are afraid to touch or think they are out of style which is the boot cut denim. Okay, wait before I go on I want to say this "Ladies there more styles of denim then just skinny, please give the skinny a break sometimes." Okay there I said it! LOL Now let's get back to our boot cut denim (Hey now), boot cut is a style that I can and will say everybody type can wear, because the flare at the bottom isn't that big where it can offset anything going on in your outfit. It will add balance to any top that you prefer to wear, tight, flowy, oversized, halter, one shoulder, you name it, boot cut works with it. If you are hippy bootcut works best for you because it has just enough flare to balance it out. I don't understand why women have put this style on the back burner when it is and should be the go to denim. It will always give your body a slender look no matter what kind of body type you have the boot cut will always work for you, even if you wear it with a heel, wedge or flat it will work. So, when in doubt always go boot cut, trust me you will begin to love them.

This time I am going to be speaking about my not so favorite style of denim and that's not because it isn't a great style, it just isn't a great style for me and that is the straight leg denim. Again, it's a great style of denim it really is, but it doesn't work for all body types. Why, they don't work for all body types is because the bottom is straight, so it doesn't balance out or take anything away from my broad shoulders. Please don't get me wrong wearing straight leg denim is in style and they are great if you are going to a networking event around other business professionals. Believe me, I wear them to networking events, but since they don't work that well for me, I need to style them accordingly. Normally when I am wearing straight leg denim, I pair them with something oversize or long, I want to take the attention away from the being straight. Not mention I also always wear a pump with them instead of any other type of heel. What this does, is create the balance I am trying to give the denim. The oversized top and pump take away from the straight denim, and people don't even notice it, they will compliment more when I do this.

Straight leg denim work for hourglass, pear and diamond body types, because the body symmetry already has/gives balance to the straight leg denim. As far as inverted triangle body types, these don't look good on us because they aren't an oversize bottom or a tight fitted bottom so it's giving our top the correct balance it needs. Rectangle and apple body types, I won't recommend this denim to you either because it will not give you any balance or emphasize anything on your body type. Now, ladies please don't get discouraged because even though they may not work for you, there is always a way to make it work. If you absolutely love the straight leg denim, you can always try to pair with different tops, you can even do a shirt dress and roll the bottom up (I do this all the time). So just because they really don't flatter my body type doesn't mean I don't make them work for me, because I do. Again, going with something oversized or long on the top usually always works, especially paired with a pump.

Lastly, I am going to be speaking about everyone's favorite go to denim, which is the skinny leg denim. YAYY!! Ladies I know that it's your favorite and I must say that it does work for all body types, but please let's style them correctly. Yes, I know they are easy and very quick to just grab and do, they can be worn with any kind of foot wear, what we pair it with on top really does matter. When you say skinny, t-shirt, button down, oversized, flowy, and cropped comes to mind, because they all give skinny leg denim balance. It also gives your body type balance and offsets the things you don't want to be seen. So since I named a few tops that work with the skinny leg denim, I am going to name a few that actually don't and they are Cami, tank tops and halter tops, "why?", because they don't give correct balance to the skinny leg denim. I know some women are mad right now because they wear skinny leg denim and Cami's all the time, but this is so wrong!! It's like being a stick because trying to find the flow of the outfit when you pair those tops with skinny leg denim just doesn't happen. Again, please don't get me wrong or be upset with me when I say that but it's funny how skinny leg denim works for all body types but just one style of shirt can offset the whole thing.

I hope that you ladies are really taking in this information and really loving it, because it all plays a part in birthing your style, you need to have denim down packed. There is more style out there than just skinny and that's just what it is. Once you get familiar with the different styles' try them and add balance to them you will find a denim that fits your style. My style is flare, do I wear flare everyday "no" but I know that flare is my style. Flare makes me feel like a grown woman for some strange reason, again I'm not saying that I don't wear other styles of denim; but I know what my style is so, I truly hope that you embrace/birth your style and learn what denim consist with your style.

Ladies,

I know we all have that one style of dress that we always wear
because it works well with our body type and we love the style of it,
while in the meantime there are so many other dresses waiting to
be worn by us too. The reason this happens is because although we
may not wear dresses all the time or we stick to that one main
dress, there is always that one dress we absolutely stay away from
no matter what, be it maxi, halter, flowy or peplum we stay far
away. One of those types of dresses we all hate, and we would never
wear it even if it was all we had. So, starting right now at this very
moment we are going to switch up your favorite dress, so there will
be no more no's and I don't like that dress.

The Maxi dress is a fitted dress and it squeezes those curves and I
think that's why some of us say "nope", I'm not wearing that," well
at least that's what I say. I absolutely adore the maxi dress and yes, I
want it to fit nicely but I don't want it to be as tight, so you know
what I do? I size up, which still gives me the fitted look, but it also
gives me room to breathe, be comfortable and enjoy the dress. You
will be amazed at what going one size up can do, so please don't be
afraid of it.

The halter dress shows your top business, especially if you are top
heavy, and that is why some women shy away from it, to keep from
tugging at it all day. Which is completely understandable because
with this dress you can't just size up, because it all depends on the
size of your breast. So, what I do and what I have done in the past to
avoid that problem and to actually feel more comfortable is I wear a
tank or a Cami and sometimes even a short sleeved shirt, believe me
I am the queen of doing that. Because I don't have to tug and left all
day and be uncomfortable checking if something is hanging out, so if
that's you too try putting something under it.

Now when it comes to the flowy dress that always makes you look
and feel bigger then you are, women tend to shy away from it

because we don't like to look bigger then what we are (that I do know). I can honestly say that's how I used to feel too until one day I put on a denim vest with it and then it became the perfect dress. Because it wasn't as flowy in the middle area with the denim vest on it and it gave it some actual shape. Now it doesn't always have to be a denim vest, it can be a denim jacket, a cardigan or even a blazer. You just want to give the dress some type of form, so it can fit your body correctly and you aren't looking bigger then you really are.

The peplum dress is really the perfect dress if you ask me because it hides the mid-section very well, it also gives off that balance that we are always looking for because where the flare starts to come out at is adding balance to our top proportion. So, no matter how we wear the peplum dress we will always have balance with it.

Ladies, I urge you to start switching up your favorite dress with these dresses and try to include the suggestions above, I think your view of your favorite dress will start to change and you will want to add more dresses to your favorite dress. Let these suggestions change your view on these dresses from horrible to fabulous and oh so chic!!!

Giving Your Body the Shape You Want

Ladies,

I know there are time that we have those moments looking in the mirror and we want to give our body another shape or give some parts a different definition. Did you know that you can do these things with simple piece?

We are going to start off with my ultimate favorite essentials which are the Mid-rise and High Waist Denim. The reason I love them so much is because they lift my butt and make it look nice and round. Can you tell a butt is something I lack in? But who cares, that's why I buy Mid-rise and High Waist Denim. LOL!

The second piece of clothing that helps is a V-neck shirt, because they make the boobs look a little bigger than what they really are. I'm not saying an extremely deep V-neck shirt, we still want to be ladies, but the V-neck does help tremendously. It falls at the right part of your cleavage to where they bring it together and make it look very nice and sexy, worn correctly.

The last piece of clothing that help is a flowy top. I know a lot of women stay away from this, but they do work. They are great for any shape or body type. The thing about a flowy top is that you can't be afraid to size up. I say size up because with that it makes it look flowy all over and not just in the mid-section area which is why so many women tend to stray away from these types of tops. When sizing up the shirt just flows, it doesn't get tight in one-section and then flowy in another (I hate that by the way), it's flowy all over which makes you look slimmer and hides the mid-section way better.

Now, these pieces are essential to me, they help me give my body the shape I am longer for and the definition that I want for when I miss those days at the gym, and since I had the twins I have been missing a lot of days. I know for a face that they will help you also, because they aren't hard pieces at all. They are little pieces with a lot of impact when worn correctly. They also save me a ton of money to buy my fabulous footwear to match (you all know I like a nice shoe).

Again, this is me, but I do want you ladies to try these pieces as well to see how they make you fill about your body shape, and the definition it gave you and I want you tell me how it went and what it made you feel like.

Fashion people often think that they can buy all the fashion in the world and that gives them substance or makes the outfit look great. WRONG!! It's your style that gives the outfit substance. It doesn't matter about the labels, it's all about how YOU wear it. Yes, I have YOU in all caps because at the end of this book I want you to know that fashion is all about YOU! Okay, now back to the topic! There are many styles out there; edgy, conservative, sexy and many, many more. What most people desire is to have a variety of every category, which means that you can wear a piece from it category, match it with your style and own it!

So, I know you are probably reading this like "how in the heck do I find my style?" Simple, style is finding your comfortable self in the mist of trends, the colors and everything else. When you become comfortable with what and who you are that's when style comes in. Please remember everyone's style is different, the way I dress may not work for someone else and vice versa, and I am fine with that.

My style is being comfortable, I'm not doing anything extra that's going to take me out of my comfort level or through off my confidence. Because when I present myself, I always want to present myself with confidence. I am a very simple dressed topped off with a bad shoe, a nice bag and a hair that looks amazing. See, that right there works for me, because that's my personality, my comfort level, I'm able to present myself with confidence not worrying about "oh does this look okay?" Do I wear dresses? Yes! Do I wear suits? Yes! But it's always simple, something I am comfortable in and it fits me, not fitting size wise that too, but I mean fitting meaning it fits my personality.

The first thing you should do when you are discovering your style is to stop looking at other people and the way they dress because me it isn't for everybody. Second, when you are getting dressed or picking clothes out put on as many pieces that you can or want and then begin to either add or subtract pieces. Please do this while looking in the mirror if not it defeats the purpose. Third, go out and buy some white V-neck t-shirts, because they will help you get comfortable with yourself. Believe me, I live by them. You can never, and I mean never go wrong with the white V-neck tee!!

Once you begin to practice these things daily, you will start to break into your comfort level, you will start to see what helps to increase your body and what decreases it, in good and bad ways. Then you know what happens style is born, that's right ladies you are birthing style. I said birthing is because style comes from the inside out, it's like love or happiness, comes from the inside first. Now they are giving birth to your style let's get ready for the compliments and very thing else to come in. You will feel comfortable, confident and you will find it easier to be yourself! Now that you have tapped into your style OWN IT AND MAKE IT YOURS!

Things that can change when you tap into our style and are extremely important, is your walk and your talk. These two things become more confident because you are feeling good about you and feeling good about how you are looking. You just put together an outfit this morning and you know you are still fly, your walk is bad and your talk is bad, why? Because that's your style, what you are wearing is fitting to your personality. When you get to this you have now surpassed Labels and fashion now you are working your style!

Making and owning your style isn't hard, all it takes is confidence. Yes, that's right I said it CONFIDENCE! This, is why style comes from the inside out, because it's a part of your confidence. That's why it's so important that you wear things that make you look great and things that you are comfortable in, because they take an effect on your confidence. So, what if I may be wearing the latest trend dress style, but if it doesn't fit my personality or go with my style when I put it on I am going to feel so uncomfortable, I'm not going to feel good about myself, I'm going to be aggravated and at the end of the night I'm going to feel defeated. I know you are wondering how this all tie into fashion and style, because first it all starts with you and how you feel, that's what makes fashion and style good or bad.

I have dressed many people and I always make sure they were comfortable with what I am putting them in. First, I would always make sure that I knew their personalities but that's for another book so I'm going to get back on topic. Yes, so where were we, owning your style will open doors to many different things inward and outward. But I am so happy that you want to take the steps to Owning your Style. I hope you are excited too because this is a journey that's going to change you fashion!

Ladies,

I truly hope you are having fun because I know that I am, but now
we are going to start bringing it home, but before we bring it on
home, I wanted to let you know there are three important pieces to
a complete outfit. They are the Classic Pieces, Basic Pieces and
Trend Pieces. When putting together an outfit you should always
have on these three pieces. Now, I know you are probably saying
"Sasha, what's the difference between them?" Well, I am so very glad
that you asked.

Classic pieces are timeless pieces, which means that they never go
out of style. They are staples to your wardrobe. Meaning that they
bring the outfit together and they make it complete. It has to be a
pretty fierce item to be a part of the classic pieces, not every item
makes the cut. But here are a few items:

- Leather Jacket
- Trench Coat
- Black Blazer
- White Button Down
- Jean Jacket
- Your perfect Denim
- The little Black Dress
- Black Trousers
- Denim Shirt
- Silk Blouse
- A-line Skirt

These are pieces that will never go out of style, and that will always
add style to your outfit. See, this is where most people miss it in
their outfit, because they won't have that staple piece and then they
are wondering why people are looking at them like something is
missing or something is just too much. The Classic piece is the
balance between it all, they bring whatever you are wearing
together. You ever see someone just through an outfit together and
then add a leather jacket or a blazer to it. They just turned a mess
into the best outfit they could have ever worn. (I know you are
laughing but it's the truth) If you want to take a mess to the best add
a classic piece.

Basic Pieces are the easy pieces. They go with everything and you can't really mess them up. If you always wear a basic piece you will always look some-what nice and put together. Why, because basic pieces are bold like the classic pieces, you know, they just chill in the outfit and don't cause too much attention, but you still know that they are there. See, that's your basic piece, I'm going to make noise but not too much, but trust me you know I am here. Here are a few basic pieces:

- T-Shirts
- Cargo Pants
- Cardigans
- Shirt Dress
- Black leggings

See how basic that was, those are your basic pieces, I'm sure if some of you are like me you probably wear a basic piece everyday (Lord knows I do), well just about. How could you go wrong with a basic piece? You can't, but oh some do, please after reading this book, please don't. It's a basic, please stop trying to make it more complicated then what it really is.

Lastly, we have the **Trend Pieces,** now these pieces are sometimes the hard pieces because they are the core of the outfit and it can either break or make it for you. See, the key to a trend piece is allowing it to stand out, that's what trend pieces do they stand out. That's why isn't never right to wear a complete outfit of trends because they are going to work against each other and then people are going to look at you like you are hurting their eyes, because they don't know what piece you want them to look at. Here are a few trend pieces:

- Peplum Top
- Color Block Dress
- Colored Jeans
- Pencil Skirt
- Floral Pants

Now these are just a few pieces, but there are a bunch of them, because they go in and out of the fashion door. One year they are in two years they are out and then boom they are back out again. Trends usually recycle every few years, that's why you will see them come in a fade out. If you have a favorite please hang on to the items because they will be back in style soon.

These are the key pieces that your outfit should consist of to be the ultimate complete. Now they always don't have to be a piece of clothing, it can be a classic shoe, a basic accessory, trendy jewelry, I mean it always varies on what you like. But you outfit should always have a Staple, a Basic and a Trend to make it stand out.

I know you are saying that's easy, but it isn't people miss it on a daily, but it is extremely important to know and apply these key pieces to your outfit, because it's what will either make your outfit or break your outfit. It will also either make your confidence or it will break your confidence as well. You know we always want to be confident in everything we wear, so let's start working more with the key pieces.

Now, let's get to the fun part!!! Yay!!

Breaking down Colors

When it comes to breaking down colors and matching them it's actually very easy, but people make it hard. Not hard as they can't comprehend but depending on the house hold you grew up in will determine the colors you may think match. If you grew up in an "old school house," you already know that blacks don't go with browns, blue and navy are different colors and your purse need to match your shoes. Wait, I am missing the most important one in an old school house" hold if you are wearing all one color and they aren't all the same shade then you don't match!

Then there's the "neutral" house hold where the only colors that exist are; white, gray, beige, cream, blue and black (which isn't consider a neutral but to them yes). Why, I said black doesn't go with everything, it goes with most of the colors but not all of them. I can hear you "Sasha are you crazy?" and my answer is "I think I just might be."

Finally, we get to the "free color" house hold which is absolutely the best house of all, why, because all the colors go together. There is no color limit in the house hold. Everyone mixes and matches colors without a care in the world.

Now, before we go any further, I am going to suggest that everyone take off the color barriers, we are going into this open-minded and ready to explore how great colors can truly be. Colors are great, and they keep you from being the "plain Jane" everyone knows what's in my closet person. I'm not saying go all out with color, not! Know the colors that work best for you and what colors you want to explore with. Because when you add just a little color to your wardrobe guess what, your whole closet changes and you are no longer in the "old school" or in the "neutral" house. You are now taking steps into the "free house" you're adding color with some of your pieces.

When it comes to matching colors we all should be living in the "free" house hold, because colors are meant to be matched with and played with. Now every color isn't for everyone so start getting familiar with your skin tone, because you don't want to wear colors that blend in with you skin tone or wash you out. You want to wear a color that bounces of your skin tone, so it will give you a vibrant and happy look. You know the look where everyone says, "girl you look great, did you do something different with your hair?" Then you would say "No, I put on a color that flourished my skin tone. With that always know that color is your best friend.

When it comes to putting an outfit together you need a color from each of those families, "the old -school," the "neutral" and the "free" household. This gives the outfit balance and substance, so you can add-on other things without losing the two. So now that you know the method of breaking down and matching colors shake off the barriers and become the "free" house hold.

Putting it all Together

We are now at my all-time favorite part, I am so excited! We are going to take everything you have read so far and create our outfit using all the essentials we have learned so far.

Before, we start grabbing our fashion pieces, let's make sure that we grab the most important thing first, which is our confidence. Grabbing our confidence first is extremely important, because it's what makes or breaks the outfit and since we are Beautiful, Fabulous and Fierce women, we always want to make the outfit! (Hey Now) Yes Ladies, I am all about making the outfit (flips hair), because you have to be confident and in love with you first and it will show through what you are wearing.

Now since we have grabbed our confidence we are ready to put together our outfit. I know it's been a long time coming but it's happening right now! Can you tell I am excited? Yes, learning how to birth your style is great, but it's nothing like putting on the outfit and having it be fierce. (lol)

First, let's walk into our closet and look around and grab our first piece, I am feeling excited so let's grab some trendy printed trousers. Yes, we are starting with the trend piece first, because the trend piece is created to stand out. That means we always want to try to pick this piece first, so we can work around it.

Next, we are going to grab a white fitted V-neck, because although I am excited right now, I'm not really feeling dressy , I feel more like being dressing comfortable. The white V-neck will be our basic piece, which will compliment and give balance to the printed trousers.

Now here comes the tricky part, because usually I always use my classics pieces for my outerwear, but today I don't plan wearing a blazer or a jacket. So today my classic piece will be my footwear. Yes, classic pieces can be footwear, accessories etc. Again, I repeat I am excited, but I am also feeling comfortable, so I am going to pick out my Red Suede Classic Pumps. You know red is my signature color! We will discuss signature colors and coloring in the next book, so for now let's get back on topic.

Since I have my, trend, basic and classics pieces all together now and the balance has been established I want everything else I include in this outfit to be as simple as possible, because I don't want to through the balance off. For my jewelry, I am going to pick out a nice simple gold watch, a nice simple chunky chain (to give my neckline some spice) and a thin bracelet. Because when it comes to jewelry always remember "Less is more", that statement is extremely true. If you over-do it with jewelry you just broke your outfit. You always want your outfit to outshine your jewelry.

We are still missing two things, which are our accessories which I want to grab two of these items, which are my purse and my shades. I want my sunglasses to be simple but fierce because I have a classic piece on my feet I want to balance it with a simple but fierce (very important) accessory.

Lastly, it's time for the ultimate accessory, and I say ultimate because the right purse is extremely important, especially when dealing with the size. Now yes ladies, I love a big oversize bag, but today that isn't the case. I already have my three key pieces on and I have my simple and fierce sunglass, so now I am going to pick out a small red over the body purse. Let's be clear that your shoes and bag doesn't have to match but something I like mine too! But let's be clear that's me! A small purse to continue the balance and the flow of our outfit. All the pieces are flowing nothing is clashing with our trend pieces which we are using as our eye catcher!

Ladies, I think it's time for us to look in the mirror and blow ourselves some kisses! You are loving you and you are loving your outfit and best of all you are loving you style. Now, we can go out walking with our heads held high, walking with confidence, speaking with confidence. We feel comfortable with what we have one and we are ready to show our outfit and new confidence to the world! LET'S GO GET IT!!!

Hey Ladies,

So, I thought since I have been speaking on birthing your style and how to create it, I thought it would be a good idea to let you in on some of my style secrets that make up my style. I am not going to lie, it took my years to birth my style and although it still evolves I know what direction I want to go in. I remember when I was in college, me and dressing could not get it together and it would make me feel bad, because of course my major was Fashion and here I am still trying to figure out what stage or level of fashion works for me. The other student would always compliment my simple dress with a fabulous shoe or handbag. That time I really didn't think anything of it, but years later down the line I am still dressing simple and dressing simple is kind of like my signature. I never want to be too much. But dressing simple matched with a fabulous shoe or a handbag is my thing and it's my style and I absolutely love it. So, when I am shopping I always keep that in mind, even when I want to try new things it's always something that's in the back of my head. Now don't get me wrong I did say that my style is evolving and since it is, my style level constantly changes, but it always remains simple, but now I am taking it to simple and fierce, why? Because I want to! LOL But, again I am still sticking with simple.

So here are some things that are in my closet, they add to my style and they're a must for me.

- White V-neck Tee
- Denim Shirts
- White Button Downs
- Oversize T-shirts
- T-Shirts
- Blazers (any color and any style)
- High waisted Denim
- Boyfriend Denim
- Cargo pants
- Trousers
- Ripped Denim

- Flowy Dresses
- Vest
- Flare Denim

I know I didn't mean a color or type but believe me when it comes to colors I am all over them. I love colors, I love wearing colors, don't get me wrong I have my fair share of black pieces but I love colors. Right now, I have on neon green sandals as I type this so yes, I love colors and not to mention my glasses are red!

My whole purpose of writing this book was to help you ladies the way I helped myself. You know it took me some time to get to know myself and get to know and be comfortable with my style. You know I was trying for years to fit in with every other style and it just wasn't working for me. I would be uncomfortable, I wouldn't feel right and everything about it, just didn't feel right. One day I told myself "why don't you just be you" and from that day I started out trying to figure out what my style was, what was I comfortable in, what fit my personality and etc. , I actually had to acknowledge what I was trying and doing wasn't working and then I had to actually take steps to make it work. Please don't get me wrong I still struggle with my style but it isn't the same struggles as before.

I know you ladies have heard the saying "Less is more" and I know some of you don't believe that. But I am here to tell you that it's the truth. Less is always more because it just looks fierce on its own. You should never have to force anything when it comes to your personality or your style of dress, it should just flow naturally and if it's not flowing naturally then you are on the wrong track and I want you to be on the right track.

So, I am going to challenge you to go out there and find your favorite pieces, find those items that you must have and please don't go by the trends, go by how you want to dress and then proceed from there. Following trends is an epic fail because people never learn about themselves, because they are always following the trends, so when you are doing this challenge please stop asking yourself what's in and what's out, because when it comes to style it's always in!!!

I hope you enjoyed taking a sneak peek into my style and some of the pieces that make it for me, I know you read that saying" those are so simple" yes, they are, because I have a simple a fierce style that works for me so everything I have is not too much! I will always make simple look fierce because it's my style, it just flows naturally when I get dressed and that works for me. I always try to take my simple style to another level, but it always stays with the keyword "Simple."

Simple is me and I accepted that a long time ago and I just allow my style to be simple and fabulous and I hope that one day you ladies will feel and do the same. Just let your style speak for its self and you feel much better about yourself. **You know it's all about loving who you are and loving your style!!!**

Conclusion

Ladies, Ladies, Ladies,

I truly hope that you enjoyed this book and had fun with it, just like I enjoyed and had fun writing it. Birthing and loving your style is a great feeling, especially when you feel good about yourself. Style is all about loving you first, loving who you are, loving you are aren't, loving your journey's just all love that involves you. Yes, I love fashion, but I enjoy showing and telling the world about my style. Because it's mine and no one can take it from me. Someone may have a similar style to mine, but it's not like mine. So yes, we all fashion, but fashion always looks the same. We want to show your confidence, show our sexiness and show our beauty in all different ways. That's what style does, it allows you to show who you are no matter what fashion you have on. You may be dressed up or dressed down, but you are comfortable and confident and showing your style.

If you have learned anything from this book, I hope that you learned how to love your body and how to love your style. Those two are very important! And don't worry we are going to be discussing many more things! This was just the Beginning.

So, let's be bold, be confident, be comfortable and be beautiful!!!

Love you

Sasha B

About Author

Sasha B

Find Author

@thesimpleandchicjunkie

Contact

Email: Lovingyourstyle29@gmail.com